MATTER and MATERIALS

EXPERIMENTS

First published in 2011 by Miles Kelly Publishing Ltd
Harding's Barn, Bardfield End Green, Thaxted, Essex, CM6 3PX, UK

This edition printed in 2015

2 4 6 8 10 9 7 5 3

Publishing Director Belinda Gallagher
Creative Director   Jo Cowan
Editors   Amanda Askew, Claire Philip
Editorial Assistant   Lauren White
Designers   Joe Jones, Kayleigh Allen
Cover Designer   Simon Lee
Photographer   Simon Pask
Production   Elizabeth Collins, Caroline Kelly
Reprographics   Stephan Davis, Thom Allaway,
Anthony Cambray, Jennifer Cozens, Lorraine King
Assets   Lorraine King

ISBN 978-1-78209-422-7

Printed in China

British Library Cataloguing-in-Publication Data
A catalogue record for this book is available from the British Library

ACKNOWLEDGEMENTS
The publishers would like to thank the following
sources for the use of their photographs:
Shutterstock.com COVER Ohn Mar; 7(tr) Sean Gladwell,
(c) Brian A Jackson, (br) travis manley, (bl) fatbob; 11(c) Yobidaba,
(tr) AdamEdwards, (br) Rtimages

Every effort has been made to acknowledge the source
and copyright holder of each picture. Miles Kelly Publishing
apologises for any unintentional errors or omissions.

Miles Kelly Publishing is not responsible for the accuracy or
suitability of the information on any website other than its own.
We recommend that children are supervised while on the Internet
and that they do not use Internet chat rooms.

Made with paper from a sustainable forest

www.mileskelly.net   info@mileskelly.net

MATTER and MATERIALS EXPERIMENTS

Chris Oxlade

Consultant: John Farndon

Miles Kelly

CONTENTS

A material can be described by its properties, such as its colour or strength.

Experiment time!

What shape are salt crystals?
Find out on page 15.

Do oil and water mix?
Find out on page 18.

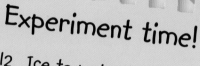

What does bleach
do to coloured water?
Find out on page 27.

Notes for HELPERS

Help and hazards

Help needed

- All of the experiments are suitable for children to conduct, but they will need help and supervision with some. This is usually because the experiment requires the use of a hob or oven, a knife or scissors, or food colouring. These experiments are marked with a 'Help needed' symbol.

- Read the instructions together before starting and help to assemble the equipment before supervising the experiment.

- It may be useful to carry out your own risk assessment to avoid any possible hazards before your child begins. Check that long hair and any loose clothing are tied back

- Also check that materials such as bleach are disposed of safely, and that the oven or hob is turned off after use.

Extra experiments

Also try...

You can also help your children with the extra experiments in this book, or search the Internet for more, similar ideas. There are hundreds of science experiment websites to choose from.

www.kids-science-experiments.com This website is packed with simple, fun experiments for your children to enjoy.

www.sciencebob.com/experiments/index.php Engaging science experiments with clearly explained instructions will keep your kids busy for hours.

www.tryscience.org You will find lots of entertaining and informative experiments on this colourful, interactive website.

pop!
pop!
pop!

bubbly

5

What is MATTER?

Matter makes up everything you can see, from the water in your glass, to the chair you are sitting on. It also makes up some things you cannot see, such as the air you breathe. There are three states of matter, which make up nearly every substance in the Universe.

The three states of matter

Everything around us is either a solid, liquid or gas, made up of billions of units called atoms. Atoms are some of the smallest objects that exist, and are invisible. Two or more atoms joined together make up a molecule. Groups of molecules make up a substance.

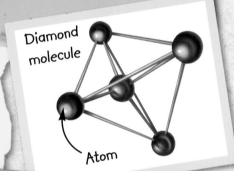

Diamond molecule

Atom

Changing state

A substance can change from one state to another by gaining or losing energy, in the form of heat.

Solid

Atoms or molecules in a solid cannot move. They are tightly packed together, so they keep their shape and feel firm.

If a liquid is cooled, it turns into a solid. This is called freezing.

If a solid is heated, it turns into a liquid. This is called melting.

Liquid

In a liquid, atoms or molecules can move or flow, but they stay the same distance apart. The links between the molecules are weaker than in a solid. A liquid can flow and fill the shape of its container.

If a gas is cooled, it turns into a liquid. This is called condensing.

If a liquid is heated, it turns into a gas. This is called evaporation.

Gas

Atoms or molecules in a gas move quickly and in all directions. The molecules bounce around because the forces between them are not strong enough to keep them together.

What are MATERIALS?

Every substance is made from a material, or a combination of materials. A material's properties, such as strength or flexibility (bendiness), make it useful for different things. Modern materials can be natural, or synthetic (chemically man-made).

Natural resources

Since ancient times, a large number of everyday materials have been made from plants, such as cotton and wood. Natural materials such as these need to be recycled (made into new things) and re-used, so they do not run out.

Wood

There are many different types of wood, varying in strength, colour, and weight. Wood comes from trees and is mainly used for fuel, or in construction (building).

Chair

Elastic bands

Rubber

Natural rubber is made from milky sap, called latex, found in some tropical trees. However, it can also be made synthetically. Rubber is flexible, tough and waterproof, which makes it useful for making car tyres.

Synthetic substances

Plastic, steel and glass are examples of synthetic materials. Sometimes a mixture of both natural and synthetic materials can be used – for example in clothing.

Drinks bottle

Plastic

Waterproof, long-lasting and strong, this synthetic material is mainly made from substances found in petroleum (crude oil). Plastics can be easily shaped and moulded and so are used in many everyday products.

Rope

Polyester

This synthetic material is often used to make clothing, as it dries quickly and holds its shape well. Rope is also often made from polyester because it is very strong.

7

USING this book

Each experiment has numbered instructions and clear explanations about your findings. Read through all the instructions before you start an experiment, and then follow them carefully, one at a time. If you are not sure what to do, ask an adult.

Experiment symbols

① Shows how long the experiment will take, once you have collected all the equipment you need.

② Shows if you need to ask an adult to help you with the experiment.

③ Shows how easy or difficult the experiment is to do.

① 30 min   ② Help needed   ③ Tricky

Introduction
See what you will be learning about in each experiment.

Things you will need
You should be able to find the equipment around the house or from a supermarket. No special equipment is needed. Always ask before using materials from home.

SALTY to fresh water

Can you separate the salt and water in salty water? Yes, by distillation – try this experiment to see how.

You will need
- work surface
- hob
- water
- glass
- table salt
- teaspoon
- small dish
- saucepan
- kitchen foil
- ice cubes
- jug

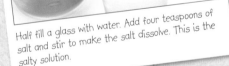

ⓐ Half fill a glass with water. Add four teaspoons of salt and stir to make the salt dissolve. This is the salty solution.

ⓑ Pour most of the salty water into a saucepan. Then stand a small dish in the centre.

There should be no water in this dish

ⓒ Put a piece of Kitchen foil over the top of Gently press down the centre of the foil s to make a dip. Put a few ice cubes in the

22

Safety
If there is a 'Help needed' symbol at the start of the experiment, you must ask an adult to help you.

The warning symbol also tells you to be careful when using Knives or scissors, or heat. Always ask an adult for help.

Stages
Numbers and letters guide you through the stages of each experiment.

Doing the experiments

* Clear a surface to work on, such as a table, and cover it with newspaper if you need to.

* You could wear an apron or an old t-shirt to protect your clothing.

* Gather all the equipment you need before you start, and tidy up after each experiment.

* Ask an adult to help you when an experiment is marked with a 'Help needed' or warning symbol.

* Work over a tray or sink when you are pouring water.

* Always ask an adult to help you if you are unsure what to do.

d

Put the pan on the hob and heat it very gently. Allow the water to boil for a few minutes (but make sure all the solution does not boil away). Be careful as the water will get hot.

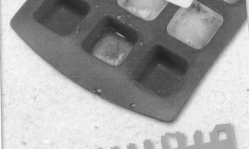

e

Make sure the dish is cold before you touch it

Remove the saucepan from the hob and leave it for one hour to cool completely. Then remove the foil. There should now be water in the dish. Taste the water in the pan and the water in the dish.

Q Do the waters taste different?

A Yes, the water in the dish is fresh water – free of salt. The water evaporated (turned to steam), leaving the salt behind in the pan, but the steam condensed (turned to water) on the cold foil and the water dripped into the dish. This process is called distillation and it is used to get fresh water from sea water.

Explanation
At the end of each experiment is a question-and-answer explanation. It tells you what should have happened and why.

Also try...

In the experiment on distillation, you removed the salt from the water and kept the water.

If you just want to keep the salt, put a saucer of the salty water in a warm place. The water will slowly evaporate, leaving the salt behind.

Also try...
Simple mini experiments test the science you've learnt.

Labels
Handy labels will provide you with useful tips and information to help your experiment run smoothly.

23

9

Scientist KIT

Before you begin experimenting you will need to gather some equipment. You should be able to find all of it around the house or from a local supermarket. Ask an adult's permission before using anything and take care when you see a warning sign.

From the craft box

- coloured pencils
- felt-tip pens (water soluble)
- lead pencils
- pencil sharpener
- sticky tape
- thick card
- thin card

Pencils

Card

From the kitchen

- chopping board
- colander
- funnel
- glasses
- jars
- jug
- kitchen foil
- kitchen towel
- knife
- saucepan with lid
- saucers
- scissors
- sieve
- small dish
- tablespoons
- teaspoons
- thermometer
- washing-up bowl
- wooden spoon

Scissors

Handy hint!
Ice cubes and frozen peas will melt very quickly. Leave them in the freezer until you are ready to use them.

Ice cubes

Funnel

Foody things

- bicarbonate of soda
- cooking oil
- flour
- food colouring
- ice cubes
- lemon juice
- milk
- peas
- red cabbage
- table salt
- tea bag
- vinegar
- water

Warning!
Scissors and Knives are extremely sharp and can cut you easily. Make sure you ask an adult for help. When passing scissors or a Knife, always point the blunt end towards the other person.

Tea bag

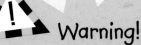

Other stuff

- 9V battery
- balloon
- Epsom salts
- filter paper
- household bleach
- petroleum jelly
- short sticks
- small plastic drinks bottle

Petroleum jelly

Balloons

Warning!

Bleach can be dangerous if not used correctly. Ask an adult for help and if you get any on your skin, be sure to wash it off immediately with water.

Places you'll need to work

- fridge
- hob
- oven
- work surface

Warning!

Be careful not to burn yourself on the hob. Remember it is hot enough to cook food on! Ask an adult for help.

Remember to recycle and re-use

One way to help the environment is by recycling and re-using materials such as glass, paper, plastics and scrap metals. It is mostly cheaper and less wasteful than making new products from stratch.

Re-using means you use materials again in their original form rather than throwing them away.

Recycling is when materials are taken to a plant where they can be melted and re-made into either the same or new products.

Peas

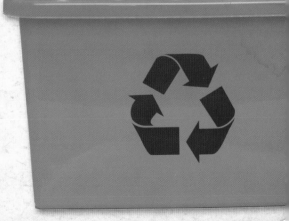

Handy hint!

Plastic bottles come in many different colours. Try to use a clear bottle so that you can see your experiment working.

11

ICE TO water to steam

Ice, liquid water and steam are just water, but in solid, liquid and gas forms. Solids, liquids and gases are the three states of matter. This experiment shows that water has different properties in each of the three states.

15 min

Help needed

Easy

You will need

- hob
- saucepan with lid
- wooden spoon
- ice cubes
- thermometer that measures from 0°C to 100°C

1b

Gently heat the saucepan and stir the ice. Ask an adult to help you heat the water on the hob because it will become hot. When the ice has begun to melt, test the temperature of the water with the thermometer.

1a

Put a saucepan on the hob and cover the bottom of the saucepan with ice cubes. Press on the ice cubes with the wooden spoon and watch what happens.

Q Does the ice flow?

A No, at first the solid ice doesn't flow or change shape. As the temperature of the water rises, it changes state – from solid ice to liquid water. This change from solid to liquid is called melting, and for ice, it normally happens at 0°C.

2a

Keep heating and melting the ice until you have liquid water. Look at how the liquid is different to the solid.

2b

Turn up the heat. Ask an adult to help you test the temperature again to see if it has changed.

3

Extreme steam!

Soon you will see bubbles forming – the liquid water is turning to steam. Put a lid on the pan and turn off the heat before all the water is gone. You should have a pan full of steam. Don't touch the pan as the steam will be very hot.

Q What does the steam do?

A The steam fills the saucepan. If you were to remove the lid, it would escape. The liquid water has changed to steam. This change of state is called boiling. For water, it normally happens at 100°C.

Q Does the water flow?

A Yes, the liquid water flows. It changes shape and flows to fill the bottom of the saucepan.

CREATE crystals

Have you ever looked really closely at table salt or sugar? If so, you've already seen crystals. Here's how to grow some crystals of your own.

15 min preparation 3 days for results   Help needed   Hard

You will need

- work surface
- oven
- fridge
- table salt
- Epsom salts
- 2 glasses
- jug
- 2 teaspoons
- 4 saucers
- water
- optional: food colouring

Preparation

Half fill two glasses with warm water. Add a few teaspoons of table salt to one glass and a few teaspoons of Epsom salts to the other glass. Stir the water in each glass so that the salts dissolve. These are your salt solutions. You could add a few drops of food colouring for fun.

1a

Don't add too much solution to the water

Pour a little table salt solution onto two saucers. Leave one saucer in a warm place. Examine the crystals after one hour, then at regular intervals for about three days.

1b

Ask an adult to put the other saucer in the oven at 140°C/275°F/GM 1 for about 15 minutes or until all the water has evaporated. Carefully remove the crystals from the oven and examine them.

Q What shape are the crystals?

A **The table salt crystals look like cubes.** They are called cubic crystals. In the solution you made, the tiny particles of table salt were mixed with water. As the water evaporated in the air or oven, the particles joined together to make crystals. Crystals have straight edges and flat faces because the particles are arranged in a neat, regular way.

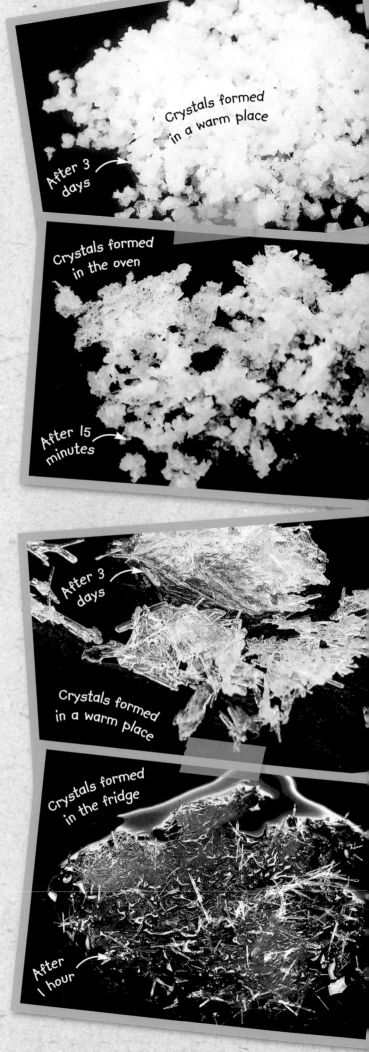

Crystals formed in a warm place

After 3 days

Crystals formed in the oven

After 15 minutes

Crystals formed in a warm place

After 3 days

Crystals formed in the fridge

After 1 hour

2a

Pour some Epsom salt solution onto two saucers. Put one saucer in a warm place and examine the crystals at regular intervals for a few days.

2b

Put the other saucer in the fridge. Examine the crystals after 10 minutes, 30 minutes and one hour.

Q Are the Epsom salt crystals different?

A **Yes, the Epsom salt crystals are needle shaped.** Just like the cubic crystals, they have straight edges and flat faces.

15

Mixing like MAGIC

Materials are made of millions of tiny particles. This experiment shows that in a liquid, the particles are constantly jiggling and moving.

15 min preparation 30 min for results

Help needed

Tricky

You will need

- work surface
- petroleum jelly
- 2 clean, empty jars
- food colouring
- water
- spoon
- jug
- piece of thin card
- washing-up bowl

a

Make the jelly really thick

Smear plenty of petroleum jelly around the rims of the two jars to make a watertight seal.

c

Fill the other jar with water, right to the top, too.

b

Half fill one of the jars with water, add a few drops of food colouring and stir. Then fill the jar with water, right to the brim.

d

Make the card 2 cm bigger than the jar

Cut a square of thin card, large enough to cover the opening of one of the jars. Put the card on top of the jar with coloured water in it.

(e)

The openings of the jars need to line up so the water doesn't leak out

Place the jar of clear water in a washing-up bowl. With one hand supporting the card, carefully turn over the jar of coloured water. Slowly slip out your hand and place the top jar on the bottom jar. You might need some help with this. Leave the jars to settle for 10 minutes before moving on to step f.

(f)

While holding the top jar steady, slowly and carefully slide out the card. Again, you might need some help with this step.

Dark red...

lighter...

light red!

Clear...

darker...

light red!

After 1 minute

After 10 minutes

After 30 minutes

Q What happens to the coloured water?

A It mixes with the clear water. The tiny water molecules are tightly packed together and are constantly moving. The water molecules from the two jars slowly mix together, carrying the particles of food colouring with them.

Can you MIX IT?

Many materials are made by mixing other materials. In these experiments, you'll put two different materials in the same container to see that some mix well and others don't mix at all.

15 min   No help needed   Easy

You will need
- work surface
- 5 jars
- cooking oil
- water
- 5 spoons
- table salt
- flour

1

Put some water and cooking oil into a jar and stir with a spoon.

2

Add salt or sugar

Half fill a clean jar with water, add a spoonful of salt and stir.

Q Do oil and water mix?

A No matter how much you stir, the oil and water don't mix. After stirring, they quickly separate again, leaving a layer of oil on top of the water. This is because the particles of oil and the particles of water repel each other.

Q Do salt and water mix?

A Yes, when you mix salt with water, the salt seems to disappear. In fact, it dissolves – it breaks into tiny particles that mix with the water. The mixture is called a solution.

3

Use a clean jar and mix a spoonful of flour into half a jar of water.

4

Pour some cooking oil into a clean jar. Add a few pinches of salt to the oil and stir.

Q Do flour and water mix?

A Yes, flour and water mix. Unlike oil and water, flour mixes much better and forms a paste. This is because the water and flour do not repel each other.

Goooey!

5

Add as much salt as possible →

Half fill a clean jar with water, add five spoonfuls of salt and stir. Add another five spoonfuls and keep stirring.

Q How much salt will dissolve?

A Lots! Eventually you will not be able to make any more salt disappear into the water. There are no water particles free to break up any more salt.

Leftover salt ↓

Q Do oil and salt mix?

A No, the salt does not dissolve. Instead it just sinks to the bottom. This is because the oil does not break up the salt crystals like water does.

19

SPLITTING the mix

A mixture is made up of two or more different materials mixed together. Sometimes you may want to separate the materials in a mixture.

30 min | No help needed | Hard

You will need

- work surface
- 3 clean, empty jars
- water
- teaspoon
- tea bag
- table salt
- peas (frozen or fresh, not tinned)
- colander
- washing-up bowl
- kitchen towel or filter paper

Preparation

Half fill three jars with water. Add some frozen or fresh peas to the first jar. Add the tea leaves from a tea bag to the second jar. Stir two teaspoons of salt into the third jar.

①

Place a colander over a washing-up bowl. Pour half the mixture of water and peas into the colander.

Q Can you separate the peas?

A Yes, you can. The colander's holes are small enough to trap the peas.

Pour half the mixture of tea leaves and water through the colander, and then half the mixture of salt and water.

Put a piece of kitchen towel in the colander. Pour the rest of the the tea and water mixture through.

Ⓠ **Can you separate tea or salt?**
Ⓐ **No, they both stay with the water.** The colander's holes are too large to trap tea leaves or salt particles.

Use clean kitchen towel

Put a new piece of kitchen towel in the colander. Pour the rest of the salt and water mixture through the paper. Dip your finger in the water and taste it.

Ⓠ **Does a filter stop the tea leaves?**
Ⓐ **Yes, it does.** The kitchen towel has very small holes between the paper fibres. They are small enough to trap the tea leaves, but not the water.

Ⓠ **Can you filter salt from water?**
Ⓐ **No, the filter paper lets salt water through.** This is why the water tastes salty. The particles of salt water are extremely tiny and easily pass through the holes.

21

SALTY
to fresh water

Can you separate the salt and water in salty water? Yes, by distillation – try this experiment to see how.

30 min | Help needed | Tricky

You will need

- work surface
- hob
- water
- glass
- table salt
- teaspoon
- small dish
- saucepan
- kitchen foil
- ice cubes
- jug

(a) Half fill a glass with water. Add four teaspoons of salt and stir to make the salt dissolve. This is the salty solution.

(b) There should be no water in this dish

Pour most of the salty water into a saucepan. Then stand a small dish in the centre.

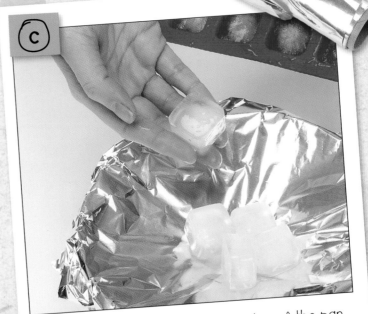

(c) Put a piece of kitchen foil over the top of the pan. Gently press down the centre of the foil slightly to make a dip. Put a few ice cubes in the dip.

d

Put the pan on the hob and heat it very gently. Allow the water to boil for a few minutes (but make sure all the solution does not boil away). Be careful as the water will get hot.

e

Make sure the dish is cold before you touch it

Remove the saucepan from the hob and leave it for one hour to cool completely. Then remove the foil. There should now be water in the dish. Taste the water in the pan and the water in the dish.

Q Do the waters taste different?

A **Yes, the water in the dish is fresh water – free of salt.** The water evaporated (turned to steam), leaving the salt behind in the pan, but the steam condensed (turned to water) on the cold foil and the water dripped into the dish. This process is called distillation and it is used to get fresh water from sea water.

Also try...

In the experiment on distillation, you removed the salt from the water and kept the water.

If you just want to keep the salt, put a saucer of the salty water in a warm place. The water will slowly evaporate, leaving the salt behind.

COLOUR separation

Inks, food colouring and dyes are often mixtures containing different colours called pigments. Try this experiment to separate pigments so that you can see what they are.

30 min | No help needed | Hard

You will need

- work surface
- 4 strips of filter paper, 2 cm by 10 cm
- water
- 4 clean, empty jars
- 4 pencils or short sticks
- sticky tape
- 4 water-soluble felt-tip pens or food colouring
- scissors
- water
- jug

ⓐ Wrap a strip of filter paper around each of your four pencils, so the paper is as long as your jar is tall. Stick it to the pencil with sticky tape.

Trim any excess paper

ⓑ Put about 2 cm of water in each of the four jars.

 What happens to the dots?

A The colours spread out and separate.
The filter paper strips soak up the water. The water picks up the different pigments in the ink and carries them upwards through the paper. The water on the paper slowly evaporates, and this draws more water upwards. Different pigments are carried different distances up the paper, and so are separated.

Use plenty of food colouring or ink

About 2 cm from the end of each strip, either draw a large dot with a felt-tip pen or add a drop of food colouring.

After 10 minutes

green = yellow + blue

After 30 minutes

yellow – no change

blue = red + blue

Carefully lower a strip (with the coloured dot at the bottom end) into each jar, so the dot is about one centimetre above the water's surface. Examine the paper every ten minutes for an hour.

After 60 minutes

red = yellow + purple

25

CABBAGE colours

What links lemon juice and bleach? One is an acid and the other is an alkali. They are opposites. Here's an experiment to show what is acid and what is alkali – using cabbage!

30 min   Help needed   Tricky

You will need

- work surface
- hob
- red cabbage
- knife
- chopping board
- saucepan
- sieve
- 3 clean, empty jars
- washing-up bowl
- teaspoons
- lemon juice
- bicarbonate of soda
- household bleach
- water

Preparation

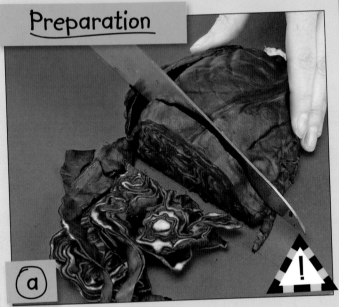

a

Ask an adult to chop half a red cabbage into small pieces.

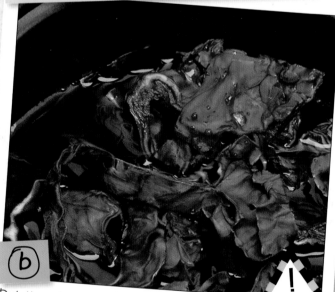

b

Put the pieces of cabbage in a saucepan and cover with water. Ask an adult to bring it to the boil and simmer for five minutes. Turn off the heat and allow the water and cabbage to cool.

c

Hold a sieve over the washing-up bowl. Pour the cabbage and water through it, so the purple water collects in the bowl.

d

Half fill the three jars with some of the purple water. The purple colour means the liquid is neutral.

1

Jar 1

Add a few drops of bleach to the first jar and stir. Ask an adult to help you pour the bleach.

Q **What does bleach do to the water?**

A It turns the purple water green, then yellow. Bleach is an alkali.

2

Jar 2

Put a few drops of lemon juice into the second jar and stir.

Q **What does lemon juice do to the water?**

A Lemon juice turns the water red. It is an acid.

3

Jar 3

Put a teaspoon of bicarbonate of soda into the third jar and stir.

Q **What does bicarbonate of soda do to the water?**

A It turns the purple colour to blue. Bicarbonate of soda is a chemical called a base, which turns water into an alkali. But it is not as alkaline as the bleach.

Bleach
Strong alkali

Lemon
Acid

Bicarbonate of soda
Weak alkali

By changing colour, the cabbage water tells us whether chemicals are acids or alkalis. It is called an indicator.

Bubbles AND FROTH

A chemical reaction is where materials are changed into new materials. Here's your chance to see chemical reactions at work.

30 min   No help needed   Easy

You will need

- work surface
- milk
- 2 glasses
- tablespoons
- vinegar
- filter paper
- funnel
- bicarbonate of soda
- small plastic drinks bottle
- balloon
- saucer

1a

Put half a cup of milk into a glass and stir in two tablespoons of vinegar. The vinegar will make the milk turn lumpy.

1c

After an hour or two, remove the pasty substance from the paper onto a saucer.

1b

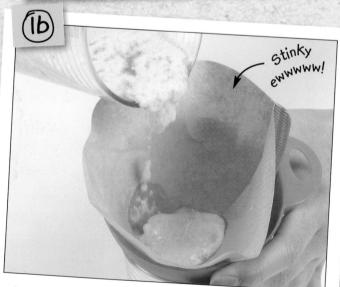

Stinky ewwwww!

Strain the mixture through filter paper into another glass. You don't need to keep the liquid.

Q What do vinegar and milk make?

A **They make a pasty substance.** A material called casein in the milk reacts with the vinegar to make a new substance, which goes hard like plastic when it dries.

Touch it, if you dare!

28

2a

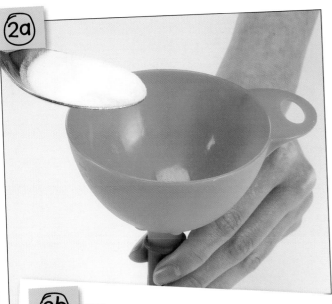

Put the narrow part of a funnel into the neck of a balloon. Carefully put two tablespoons of bicarbonate of soda into the funnel and shake it down into the balloon.

Up, up and away!

2b

Don't tip any bicarbonate of soda into the bottle yet

Add 2 cm of vinegar to the bottle. Then carefully attach the balloon to the top of the bottle.

2c

Lift up the balloon and shake it so the bicarbonate of soda falls into the bottle.

Q **What happens to the balloon?**

A **The balloon inflates!** The vinegar reacts with the bicarbonate of soda, making carbon dioxide gas. This gas fills the balloon.

ELECTRIC bubble-maker

In this experiment you send electricity through water. The electricity breaks up the water, making tiny bubbles of gas.

30 min | No help needed | Hard

You will need

- work surface
- thick card
- clean, empty jar
- 2 lead pencils, the same length
- pencil sharpener
- water
- 9V battery

a

Cut a square of thick card about 2 cm wider than the opening of the jar.

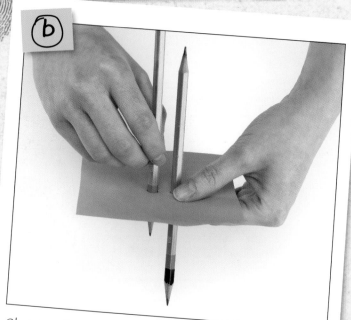

b

Sharpen both ends of the pencils. Then carefully push the pencils through the card, about 2 cm apart.

c

Don't let the pencils touch the bottom

Half fill the jar with water. Then place the card on top of the jar and slide the pencils up or down so that their ends are level and underwater.

(d)

Hold the battery upside down on top of the pencils so that the battery terminals touch the pencil leads.

Also try...

Add some salt to the water, stir it in and repeat the experiment. Sniff the air above the jar.

Can you smell chlorine or a 'swimming pool' smell? When you add salt, chlorine comes from the pencil lead attached to the positive terminal. Chlorine is one of the elements in salt (which is sodium chloride, or NaCl).

pop!
pop!
pop!

bubbly

Q Can you see bubbles?

A The small bubbles that appear on the pencil leads and rise to the surface are bubbles of **oxygen and hydrogen.** These are the two chemical elements in water. Oxygen is produced when the pencil lead touches the positive battery terminal, and hydrogen is made when the pencil lead touches the negative battery terminal.

RECORD
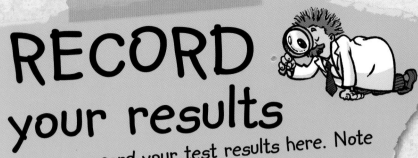
your results

You can record your test results here. Note down how successful the experiments were and what you have learnt about science from them. You could also write about how much you enjoyed each activity.

Add a picture of yourself as a scientist!

Quiz ZONE

Get ready to test how much you've learnt from the experiments in this book. Write down your answers on a piece of paper and then check them against the answers on page 40. No cheating!

Q1 picture clue

What is the missing word?

① If water is heated, it starts to change from a liquid to a ... .

② Instead of throwing away plastic and paper, we should ... .

③ If two substances will not mix, they ... each other.

④ When a gas cools and changes to a liquid, it is ... .

⑤ The process of heating water until it evaporates, then cools to become a liquid again, is called ... .

Remember, remember

⑥ At what temperature will water begin to boil?

⑦ When vinegar is added to bicarbonate of soda, which gas is produced?

⑧ Which two chemical elements make up water (H_2O)?

⑨ What shape are table salt crystals?

Q7 picture clue

True or false?

10. When oil and water are mixed together, the oil dissolves into the water.

11. Rubber is a natural material.

12. There are four states of matter.

Q10 picture clue

Multiple choice

13. When atoms or molecules are tightly packed together, and they cannot move around, what do they form? A solid, liquid or gas?

14. What is the name of the process that changes ice to water? Melting, evaporating or freezing?

15. Which of these is a natural material? Wood, plastic or polyester?

Q15 picture clue

16. What is made when salt and water mix? A solution, a reaction or a mixture?

What word beginning with...

17. F turns a liquid into a solid?

18. A is the opposite to an alkali?

Q17 picture clue

19. P makes up colours in inks, dyes and food colouring?

20. F can be used to separate a solid from a liquid?

More questions this way

PICTURE
Quiz

Kitchen paper

Colander

21 What material could you use to filter tea leaves from water?

ⓒ

Sieve

ⓑ

22 Which of the following diagrams represents a solid?

ⓐ

ⓑ

ⓒ

ⓐ

ⓑ

23 Which of the following is an alkali?

ⓑ

ⓐ

Bleach

Lemon

ⓒ

24 Which picture shows Epsom salt crystals formed in a cold place?

ⓑ

25 What will a mixture of coloured and clear water look like after 30 minutes?

ⓐ

GLOSSARY

Acid A chemical substance that has a pH level of less than 7.

Alkali A chemical substance that has a pH level of more than 7.

Atom The smallest particle of an element.

Boiling point The temperature at which a liquid bubbles and changes into a gas when it is heated.

Condensing The process of a gas changing to a liquid as it cools.

Dissolving If a solid dissolves, it mixes with a liquid and makes a solution.

Distillation The process used to separate a liquid from a solution by evaporation and condensing.

Element A simple chemical substance that consists of only one kind of atom, and can not be broken down.

Evaporation The process in which water is heated and changes from a liquid to a gas.

Filter To separate two substances in a mixture by passing it through something, such as a sieve.

Freezing point The temperature at which a liquid cools and changes into a solid.

Material What every substance is made from. Materials can be natural (e.g. wood), or synthetic (e.g. polyester).

Matter All substances are made up of very small particles, or matter, and can be a solid, liquid or gas.

Melting The process that changes a solid into a liquid, mainly when heated.

Mixture A substance that contains two or more different substances that are mixed, but not chemically bound. They can be easily separated.

Molecule At least two atoms held together by a chemical bond.

Neutral A chemical substance with a pH level equal to 7.

pH scale The measure of how acidic or alkaline a solution is.

Pigment A mixture of different colours that make up one colour when put together.

Reaction When a chemical change occurs and materials are changed into new materials. E.g. when vinegar reacts with bicarbonate of soda, carbon dioxide is made.

Repel When two or more substances do not mix.

Separation When two or more materials in a mixture are moved apart.

Solution A mixture in which a gas, solid or liquid is dissolved in a liquid.

Thermometer A piece of equipment used to measure temperature.

INDEX

QUIZ answers

1. Gas 2. Recycle 3. Repel 4. Condensing 5. Distillation 6. 100 degrees Celsius
7. Carbon dioxide 8. Hydrogen and oxygen 9. Cube shaped 10. False – they repel each other
11. True 12. False – there are three 13. Solid 14. Melting 15. Wood 16. Solution 17. Freezing
18. Acid 19. Pigments 20. Filter 21. a (kitchen paper) 22. b 23. a (bleach) 24. b 25. a